Scooterama

This edition first published in 1999 by MBI Publishing Company,
729 Prospect Avenue, PO Box 1, Osceola, WI 54020-0001 USA

The information in this book is true and complete to the best of our knowledge.
All recommendations are made without any guarantee on the part of the author
or publisher, who also disclaim any liability incurred in connection with the use
of this data or specific details.

We recognize that some words, model names and designations, for example,
mentioned herein are the property of the trademark holder. We use them for
identification purposes only. This is not an official publication.

MBI Publishing Company books are also available at discounts in bulk quantity
for industrial or sales-promotional use. For details write to Special Sales
Manager at Motorbooks International Wholesalers & Distributors,
729 Prospect Avenue, PO Box 1, Osceola, WI 54020-0001 USA.

Library of Congress Cataloging-in-Publication Data Available.

ISBN 0-7603-0789-X

Printed in Dubai

Project Editor: Roland Hall
Project Art Direction: Trevor Newman
Production: Bob Bhamra
Picture Research: Catherine Costelloe

Scooterama

Café Chic and Urban Cool

ALASTAIR WALKER

MBI Publishing Company

Lambrettability

Lambretta's mobility is an investment!

Contents

'I drew a man sitting down comfortably, with wheels underneath him … immediately a design was born'

Introduction

It was with these words that Corradino d'Ascanio, the man who was responsible for designing the very first Vespa in 1946, described how, after many sleepless nights wrestling with the problem of creating a two-wheeled mass transportation vehicle, he approached his drawing board.

ABOVE: **FOR THE YOUTH OF TODAY… THE APRILIA SPICESONIC 50**

LEFT: **… AND YESTERDAY MEMBERS OF THE LAMBRETTA CLUB GB IN THE EARLY SIXTIES**

**SCOOTERING:
FUN, YOUTH
AND FREEDOM**

The shape which came to define the word 'scooter' around the world, the ubiquitous Vespa — named after the Italian word for wasp — was a masterpiece of simplicity and Italian style. d'Ascanio's Vespa was more than basic transport, although it fulfilled that function perfectly. It came to represent fun, youthfulness and freedom. To a post-war generation fed up with ration books, petrol coupons and Dad's old demob suit, scooters were sleek, new, jet-age toys.

Two Italian companies, Piaggio and Lambretta, expanded rapidly throughout the Fifties to dominate the booming European scooter market. They hired Hollywood movie stars to advertise scooters, they helped organize clubs around the world, sponsored endurance trials, speed records, beauty pageants — did anything to sell scooters, and the glamorous lifestyle that went with them, to as many people as possible.

It worked so well that even in grey, austerity-gripped Fifties' Britain just over half the 300,000 brand-new two-wheelers sold in 1959 were scooters — a record which remains unbroken.

That mushrooming popularity, matched with the British economy of the 'Swinging Sixties', also spawned a new style amongst the younger brothers and sisters of the original rock 'n' roll generation: Mod.

The Mod generation dressed in tailored suits, read *Town* magazine, bought

Stax, Atlantic and Motown '45s, scootered to gigs by Brit groups like The Small Faces, The Kinks, The Who and many more – Sixties' teenagers, with jobs, pills, *the* Pill and a driving licence at sixteen. They wanted to escape at the weekend, dress sharp and be seen in the right places, and only one vehicle would do; the scooter. Britain was Lambretta's biggest overseas market.

In mainland Europe and elsewhere in the world, the basic demand for cheap personal transport kept many scooter manufacturers in business through another three decades. Now the wheel has turned full circle in the 1990s, as traffic volumes in choked European cities make the scooter a quicker way to get around town than anything else on wheels. It's also become a modern-age badge of retro-style cool, from Osaka to Ocean Colour Scene.

This book is a celebration of the profound impact the scooter has had on transport and popular culture in the second half of the 20th century, both as a design classic and a hi-tech commuter tool. The scooter just keeps on re-inventing itself and looks set to power another generation into the next millennium.

SCOOTERS – RE-INVENTING THE WHEEL FOR THE LAST FIFTY YEARS

Avanti!

① Roman Holiday

Europe was torn apart by the Second World War. When it finished in 1945, Enrico Piaggio surveyed the damage inflicted by the USAAF on his Pontedera aircraft factory and knew he needed a new product. He decided to commission a man who was then Italy's leading helicopter designer, Corradino d'Ascanio, to come up with a cheap, durable means of transport for the ordinary man in the street to commute upon. D'Ascanio relished the challenge and the rest, as they say, is history…

ABOVE: **TROY DONAHUE GIVES SUZANNE PLESHETTE A LIFT TO THE STUDIO IN HOLLYWOOD**

LEFT: **THE SWEET LIFE IN SAN REMO, 1964, AS THE VESPA CLUB TAKE TO THE STREETS**

THE PAPARINO PROTOTYPE SCOOTER WAS NOT WELL RECEIVED AND ENRICO
PIAGGIO ASKED D'ASCANIO TO IMPROVE THE LOOKS OF THE MACHINE

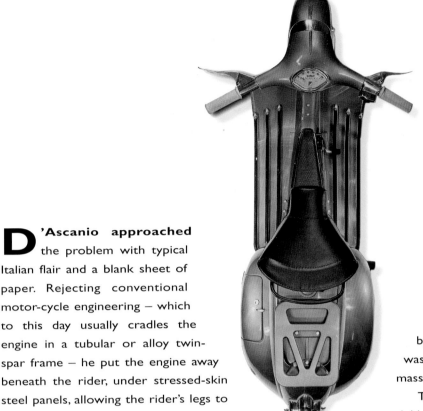

DESIGNS FOR LIFE: THE VESPA WAS SIMPLY SCULPTURE IN METAL

TAKING IT TO THE STREETS: THE ITALIAN VESPA CLUB, 1954

D'Ascanio approached the problem with typical Italian flair and a blank sheet of paper. Rejecting conventional motor-cycle engineering — which to this day usually cradles the engine in a tubular or alloy twin-spar frame — he put the engine away beneath the rider, under stressed-skin steel panels, allowing the rider's legs to be set comfortably on running-boards. The chassis followed car practice, being monocoque, constructed from one central section of steel with the 98cc engine, wheels, suspension and handle-bars all bolted on to the main unit.

At the front, there was another touch of Pontedera's aircraft heritage; a stub axle front fork with a solid dish wheel. Both wheels were identical, which meant they were interchange-able, or could be quickly replaced by a spare in the event of a flat. It was a clever, compact design, ideal for mass production.

The scooter was born in 1946, dubbed the Paparino by its creator. With it, d'Ascanio had broken the motorcycle mould; he had created the first two-wheeler for the machine age; a modern, practical, transport solution. The two-wheeled equivalent of the Volkswagen Beetle.

THE ORIGINAL VESPA 98 OF 1946. IT FEATURED A 98CC
FAN-COOLED, TWO-STROKE, SINGLE-CYLINDER
ENGINE, DRIVING DIRECTLY TO THE REAR WHEEL

Sadly, it also looked twice as ugly as a Beetle. People openly laughed at the Paparino and only about 500 were sold. Enrico Piaggio asked d'Ascanio to give his baby a stylish makeover, turning the original ponderous-looking scooter into a much sleeker, sharper vehicle. It

**VESPA PROMOTION
FROM THE SEVENTIES**

was still fairly wide and hung low to the ground, but that was because there was no stand on the Vespa. To park it, the rider merely leaned the Vespa over on to a running-board.

The story goes that the boss of Piaggio saw the new design and straight

THE SLEEK LINES AND BEAUTIFUL CURVES OF THE 1998 ET4 NOT ONLY
REFLECT THE STYLE OF EVERYTHING THE ORIGINAL 1946 VESPA STOOD
FOR, BUT PUT THE SCOOTER AT THE FOREFRONT OF TRANSPORT DESIGN

**SEVENTIES STYLE:
SIGN OF THE TIMES**

away remarked how like a wasp its profile was. The nickname stuck: the Vespa had arrived. The initial reaction elsewhere was mixed, however. The motorcycle press hated the Vespa, regarding it as an underpowered joke. But people bought it, rode it and liked its built-in convenience and practicality. In the bombsite cities of Europe, with petrol, food and other essentials still being rationed, people were in dire need of mobility. The Vespa was akin to salvation on wheels.

Enter Lambretta

The same heavy bomber damage which Piaggio suffered, coupled with American finance, enabled another Italian company to launch their personal transport solution in 1947.

Like Piaggio, the Innocenti steel tube manufacturing company near Milan had switched to war armaments production from the late 1930s to 1945. But Ferdinando Innocenti was determined to see his company prosper once more from the humble steel tube and transport was the obvious solution, the catalyst of the entire Italian *reconstruzione* process.

The Lambretta Series A, Innocenti's first scooter, was a 123cc, single-cylinder machine, with the engine set next to the rear wheel, using direct bevel gear drive. A central load-bearing tube formed the chassis backbone, with footboards fitted and a pair of legshields to protect the rider. It also had a foot-operated gearchange like a motorcycle. It was slightly more powerful than the Vespa, with a top speed of just over 40mph. Throughout their great rivalry, the Lambretta would always retain a reputation amongst scooter *cognoscenti* as the faster marque. Whilst the Lambretta Series A model may have been fast, few could claim it was stylish, with an exposed engine making the whole thing look a bit 'make do and mend'. From 1950 onwards, with the introduction of the C series, Lambrettas had a visual appearance which was almost identical to the Vespa with the engine fully enclosed with side panels, and wider legshields.

It too, was a success with the public. Both companies knew they were on to something and began selling scooters all over Europe. With petrol getting slightly easier to obtain, the 1950s offered Piaggio and Innocenti a golden opportunity to corner the market in cheap, personal two-wheeled transport. The two Italian giants pursued that dream with a vengeance.

THE FIRST LAMBRETTA, SERIES A, OFFERED VERY BASIC TRANSPORT

BY THE LATE FIFT THE LAMBRETTA WA MUCH IMPROVED

Jayne Mansfield

Lambretta

INNOCENTI

Selling The Dream

The scooter's rise as a method of mass transport was greatly encouraged by large-scale advertising campaigns for the Vespa and Lambretta marques. Both companies expanded production capacity to meet the demand, unlike most motorcycle manufacturers of the time.

Vespa France was established in 1950, with the British Vespa-Douglas forming in Bristol, England, the following year. Subsidiary companies had to follow the design of the Vespa to the letter: no modification or alteration was allowed without approval from Piaggio themselves. The customer then knew exactly what they were getting and they loved it.

Vespa-Douglas were flooded with orders at the 1950 Motor Cycle Show and

SCOOTER ADVERTISING IN THE 1950S WAS ALWAYS DIRECT. BUT IF YOU HAVE SOMETHING GOOD TO SELL, SHOUT ABOUT IT

motorcycle — that was the essence of the Fifties appeal of the scooter to the average working man, or woman.

Both companies were lucky that governments across Europe made borrowing easier in the Fifties to encourage economic growth, but the Vespa and the Lambretta were also advertised in a new, vibrant way which put motorcycle manufacturers to shame.

For the first time, the Italians took two-wheelers out of the minority-interest image 'ghetto' which motorbike manufacturers had constructed. Scooters were a mass-consumption convenience vehicle, and Piaggio and Lambretta sold their products like baked beans, pop records or washing powder. They appealed to the young, the post-war generation, with a carefree message of optimism and freedom.

went on to build 126,000 scooters over the next eight years. Demand in Italy was voracious and one million Vespas were made at Pontedera by 1956.

Lambretta too were enjoying similar success, with production runs of popular models growing from the 30–40,000 mark to as many as 110,000 by the mid-Fifties. They also pursued overseas markets, particularly the UK, Spain and Germany where large sections of the population were already experienced motorcycle riders, but not necessarily enthusiasts. The convenience of a car, at the price of a

YOU COULD GO ANYWHERE AND DO ANYTHING ON A SCOOTER

La Bonne Vie!

Go Vespa! Do The Lambret-twist

Scooter manufacturers also welcomed women as part of this new transport revolution, but companies took a dual approach in terms of imagery. Whilst women were encouraged to ride scooters because of the machine's sheer practicality, they were also used as simple sexy decorations in advertising posters, films and sales literature. The first Miss Lambretta and Miss Vespa beauty pageants took place in the early 1950s. Both companies lost no time in signing up female movie stars, and arranging an endless parade of cheesecake photography sessions with lightly-clad girls on scooters.

There were other publicity stunts, of course. Scooter clubs were encouraged to tour vast distances, set fuel economy records, ride off-road in muddy trials, meet at rallies etc. All this activity made the scooter the centrepiece of an entire lifestyle. A new, exciting image surrounded scootering in the Fifties, with feats of endurance, such as riding them up Ben Nevis or racing the Golden Arrow London-to-Paris train, all the rage.

MODELS ADDED GLAMOUR TO THE VESPA-DOUGLAS SCOOTER OF 1949

A SCENE FROM THE MOVIE *HETERO SEXUAL* WITH MIXED MESSAGES ON SAFE SCOOTERING

Hollywood

Perhaps the boldest marketing initiative was recruiting Hollywood's biggest movie stars to make scooters fashionable. Vespa made sure their scooter was ridden everywhere by Gregory Peck and Audrey Hepburn in the Oscar-winning 1953 film Roman Holiday. They also signed up stars such as Doris Day, Charlton Heston — even the Duke himself, John Wayne — to sit on a Vespa. Lambretta were equally busy in movie promotion, with Grace Kelly, Debbie Reynolds, Cliff Richard and Jimmy Cagney all getting a bit of Lambretta sponsorship. Jayne Mansfield spent hours posing on her gold-plated

SILVER SCREEN SCOOTER: (CLOCKWISE FROM TOP LEFT) RAQUEL WELCH; CHARLTON HESTON; ANTHONY QUINN'S OFFER OF A RIDE DOESN'T SEEM TO PLEASE INGRID BERGMAN; EDDIE ALBERT, GREGORY PECK AND AUDREY HEPBURN ENJOY A ROMAN HOLIDAY; DEAN MARTIN LOOKS PLEASED WITH HIS LATEST MOBILE BAR STOOL

**URSULA ANDRESS,
SIMPLY PURR-FECT
IN LEOPARDSKIN
ACCESSORIES**

Lambretta. Nobody had ever sold two-wheeled vehicles like this before. Motorcycles at the time were sold either sold as TT-winning race replicas or small-capacity, penny-pinching, utilitarian transport, suitable mainly for Brylcreemed men with a well-equipped tool shed.

But the Italians lived differently and didn't care for convention. They had style and they knew how to flaunt it. The scooter soon became the favourite accessory for anyone with a taste for *La Dolce Vita*.

CLOCKWISE FROM TOP LEFT: ANTHONY PERKINS ON HIS VESPA; JOHN WAYNE RELAXES SIDE-SADDLE; DEBBIE REYNOLDS IS *THE SINGING NUN*; ROCK HUDSON AND BOBBY DARIN RACE IN *COME SEPTEMBER*; REX HARRISON RIDES PILLION WITH RICHARD BURTON IN *STAIRCASE*

ROCK HUDSON   GINA LOLLOBRIGIDA
SANDRA DEE   BOBBY DARIN
WALTER SLEZAK in
Come September
Technicolor   Lenses by Panavision

**ONE OF VESPA'S
GREATEST TRIUMPHS:
THE GS150**

While the advertising was slick, so too was the product. Neither Piaggio nor Innocenti stopped developing new models throughout the Fifties, fuelling the curiosity of a market searching for the very latest 'mod. con'. The typical motor-cycle manufacturer of the time regarded a new paint scheme and a bored-out engine as a decade's worth of development, but Vespa and Lambretta were always looking for improvement, evolving the scooter concept.

The Vespa G series saw the cumbersome, steel rod-operated gearchange replaced by cables at the throttle. Engines increased in size; first to 125cc, then 150cc, as club members and commuters demanded more speed and power.

Lambretta followed suit, determined to stay ahead in the power race with its great rival. The TV175 series, introduced in 1957, boasted four gears, rather than just three, with a top speed approaching 65mph. Spare wheels, natty luggage carriers, chrome guard-rails all started to appear, first as options, then as standard on the ever-smarter scooter.

But there was another reason why both Piaggio and Innocenti were striving hard for dual dominance in the booming Fifties' scooter market. Competitors were beginning to wake up and other manufacturers were jumping on the bandwagon, having seen the phenomenal success of the two Italian companies.

... AND ONE OF LAMBRETTA'S: THE 'SLIMSTYLE' TV175

② Globetrotter

Although the Vespa defined the modern scooter, the basic concept of the enclosed two-wheeler had, in fact, been around since the turn of the twentieth century. Small firms, especially in Britain, France and America all tried assembling rough-and-ready vehicles in small numbers, as various solutions to the problem of motorized bicycles as clean commuting machines rather than big and dirty speed machines were tried.

LEFT: GUY FORQUET AND JANE SEBERG CRUISING THE STREETS OF PARIS

ABOVE: A WINNER IN ONE OF THE MANY 'MISS LAMBRETTA GB' CONTESTS, TAKES HER PRIZE ON A TRIP ABROAD

THE ORIGINAL GIRL POWER: AN INDEPENDENT WOMAN IN THE 1920S TRIES THE UNIBUS SCOOTER

The French Auto-Fauteuil (armchair) of 1904, which had an engine under the seat and basic footboards, was a typical pioneer example. The British company ABC had a decent go at the concept with their Skootamota of 1921, which was marketed as the ideal runabout for the high-society 'flapper' of the era. The bulky bathtub-on-wheels known as the Unibus was another British attempt from the early 1920s.

But early designs never caught on. The reason was social; most people did not need their own transport. They worked and socialized close to where they lived and the destruction caused by the First World War was much more localized than in the Second World War — heavy bombing of cities simply didn't happen, so public transport was largely unaffected.

Even in the wide open spaces of the USA, where buses were infrequent, an engine manufacturer such as Cushman failed to develop large-volume sales of their scooter during the Depression era, when people needed cheap transport. Also, cars were relatively cheap in the States in the 1930s compared with prices in Europe. Despite this, Cushman scooters had an unexpected influence on basic designs in Japan and Europe through their use by US armed forces during the Second World War.

In Turin, the Fiat car company toyed with a prototype scooter back in 1938,

LEFT: **THE BASIC CONCEPT WAS ALWAYS A RIDE-TO-WORK MACHINE. THIS MAN BEATS THE RAIL STRIKE OF 1955**

RIGHT: **THE 1921 ABC SKOOTAMOTA WAS MORE OF A TOY, A BIT LIKE A MODERN DAY MOTORIZED SKATEBOARD**

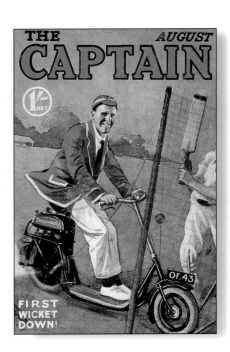

but never put their two-wheeler into production. The people who could afford personal transport usually chose a car or motorcycle. In short, the scooter was one of many pioneer transport designs which went nowhere for the first 45 years of the 20th century. Its only large-scale use was during the Second World War, when both the Cushman and the British Welbike (later to appear briefly on the post-war civilian market as the Corgi) were dropped as foldable run-abouts for paratroopers following landing. Neither was regarded as being very useful by most soldiers, as their tiny, unreliable engines usually broke down, often within minutes of starting.

French Freedom

Europe in the mid-1950s was a place of relative poverty. Petrol was still in short supply and expensive in most countries, including France. Most people walked or cycled to work, but those who could afford a scooter or motorcycle were usually concerned with economy, durability and low maintenance costs. The two-wheeler manufacturers of post-war France were mainly concerned with building motorbikes, aimed at the enthusiast. But many of them were either forced, or enlightened enough, to consider making first cycle-motors, then scooters, to grab a piece of this 'gimmick' market while it lasted in the 1950s.

At the Paris Motorcycle Show of 1954, for example, 12 French manufacturers had scooter-style vehicles on their stands. Some, like Terrot — who supplied motorcycles to the French armed forces — produced them after being encouraged by their government, alarmed at the 'Italian invasion'.

Others, like Roussey with their inventive flip-up-bodied scooter, or

Motobecane, the leading French manufacturer, took the job more seriously.

They were right to do so, as the French market had mushroomed to 975,000 new machines during that year. Of that incredible tally, something less than 40,000 two-wheelers were full-sized motorcycles; the rest were sub-200cc motorcycles, scooters or clip-on cyclemotors. The cyclemotor — which is still produced in France today and legal to ride aged 14 in France — was extremely popular, accounting for around 660,000 new sales.

Motobecane had a design prototype scooter called the Moby, created by M. Jaulmes in the early Fifties. They already dominated the small commuter market, selling an astonishing 251,000 Mobylette mopeds a year in the mid-Fifties, but they realized they needed at least one scooter in their range to cash in on the boom.

With sleeker bodywork, a tried and tested four-stroke 125cc engine, twin-saddle option and pressed-steel sections bolted to a tubular frame à la Lambretta, the SC

AT THE PARIS MOTORCYCLE SHOW OF 1954 12 FRENCH
MANUFACTURERS HAD SCOOTER-STYLE VEHICLES ON THEIR STANDS. TERROT
WERE ENCOURAGED BY THE GOVERNMENT, ALARMED AT THE 'ITALIAN INVASION.'

Leve de Vacantie!

model was born. It was called the Motoconfort, which was a subsidiary company owned by Motobecane. The Moby scooter was an immediate sales success and a two-stroke-engined model, the SB, appeared the following year, along with the more expensive SCC model, which had enhanced engine cooling vents in the main bodywork panels.

Engine cooling was a problem inherent in the design of the scooter, since an enclosed engine shut away behind panels will invariably get hot. Piaggio and Lambretta did OK with fan-assisted engine cooling, but French manufacturer Roussey took the bold step of placing a radiator in the front panel which pumped water around a horizontally mounted, 175cc two-stroke motor at the back of the scooter. The entire rear bodywork section which covered the motor hinged upwards for easy engine maintenance. The Roussey was a clever design, a distinct improvement on the basic d'Ascanio concept in several respects, yet it was let down by having a lawnmower-style pull-cord starting mechanism for the engine. Lambretta and other manufacturers were already trying out electric starters by the mid-Fifties.

Another interesting French model was the Bernadet Cabri 50, which had the alloy-constructed two-stroke engine, transmission and rear suspension unit all in one casting, linked directly to the back wheel. It meant that the compact power train could be sold to other manufacturers as a single unit.

The Cabri also had its rider sitting astride a streamlined fuel tank, which again emphasized the neatness of the whole concept. It was advertised as a scooter small enough to pack into the boot space of a car — admittedly a large American car — and it sold for just 67,000Fr (£67). Très cute.

ABOVE AND RIGHT: LIKE THE ITALIANS, THE FRENCH APPROACHED THE
MARKETING OF SCOOTERS WITH A CERTAIN SENSE OF STYLE

Germany Calling

**THE GERMAN
MAICOLETTA 250CC
SCOOTER OF 1961**

Of course, the Germans were another nation recovering from the colossal damage inflicted by the war and their motorcycle industry was quick to seize the opportunity of selling scooters. Over 20 companies manufactured scooters during the 1950s in Germany. Unsurprisingly, the nation's tradition in engineering excellence and wartime aviation technology both had a great impact on homegrown scooters, especially in their styling.

The main philosophy behind German two-wheeler scooters was

long-distance touring, rather than simply getting to work, which applied broadly to German motorcycles, scooters and bubble cars. In general, the German scooters were superbly made machines for their time, very luxurious, heavy and full of expensive features.

Early models such as the enormous Maico Mobil of 1951 demonstrated how much emphasis the German scooter designers placed on aerodynamics. The fairing looked as if it had been lifted straight from an aircraft fuselage. The Maico Mobil was sold as 'the car on two wheels' — and it was almost as heavy. Its hand-finished aluminium body panels weighed over 110 kilograms, or approximately 240lbs. That alone was more than many 350cc-class motor-cycles of the time, yet the first Maico Mobil only had a 150cc two-stroke engine. The Maico carried a huge 14-inch spare wheel at the back, had four gears, a reserve fuel supply and a red saddle made of rubber for waterproofing purposes — no wet knickers on a Maico.

A similar giant scooter, the Bastert, which was actually designed by a Frenchman, was another early-Fifties jet-age 'streamliner.' Again, it used an advanced aluminium alloy body, rather than pressed steel, but the Bastert was still slow and ungainly. Einspur Auto only made around 1,200 Bastert scooters, selling them on the premise that they were 'single-track cars' — a concept BMW would rediscover in the 1990s.

Former aircraft manufacturer Heinkel's most successful model was proba-bly the 175cc Tourist, which was one of the better four-stroke-engined German designs of the Fifties. A simple, single cylinder, overhead valve engine was ideal for holiday use, especially carrying a passenger, as the unit made around 9bhp, or around twice the power of the first Lambretta. It was also one of the very

THE RARE AND IMPRESSIVELY WELL-BUILT BASTERT SCOOTER

first scooters to have electric starting like a car, rather than the kickstart lever. The Mark Two version of the Tourist even had 12-volt electrics, a luxurious dual seat and flashing indicators. The accent was on comfort and overall build quality — a feature which sold many Heinkels in Britain, despite the recent memory of German aircraft bombers and the war.

There were some small designs, of course. The Achilles was based on the US armed forces' Cushman — which basically looked like a motorized skateboard — but the Achilles didn't catch on and the company sold out to the British Norman factory in 1957. Typewriter company Adler tried their hand with the Junior model in 1955, but it too ceased production a few years later. Small just did not sell in Germany.

The typical German scooter was very big, in every respect. The Durkopp Diana had a 200cc-class two-stroke engine and weighed 317lbs dry. It wasn't one for the ladies — unless the women in question were Olympic shotputters. The Puch Alpine 150, NSU Prima 175 and Zundapp Bella were all similar touring scooter concepts, usually featuring 12-inch diameter wheels, which gave them slower, almost unwieldy steering characteristics at low speeds, but real stability at cruising speed.

THE STREAMLINE STYLE OF THE HEINKEL TOURIST

OASIS CHOSE THE ZUNDAPP BELLA FOR THE COVER OF *BE HERE NOW*

39

The Zundapp Bella was available in two engine sizes, the 154 and 204 models. Both were two-stroke motors, but anyone who chose the small 148cc option to push their 300-odd pounds of bizarrely styled scooter would find progress on the slow side.

The problem with German scooters of the Fifties could be summed up by the Bella; although its 200cc two-stroke engine developed 13bhp, making it vastly superior in performance to the average Italian or British two-stroke motor of the time, the scooter's actual top speed was barely 60mph — exactly the same as a cheaper British, French or Italian utility machine.

By trying too hard to improve on the basic simplicity of the Vespa or Lambretta, the Germans pretty much missed the point about scooters — they were primarily designed for nipping to the shops, not visiting your cousin in Switzerland.

Brit Flops

THE PEAK IN 1959 FOR SCOOTER SALES IN THE UK CONCENTRATED MINDS IN THE BOARDROOMS OF BRITAIN, BUT IT WAS TOO LATE …

The British motorcycle industry dominated the world in the 1950s, egged on by government instructions to 'export or die'. But British bike manufacturers regarded scooters as a cheap novelty, mainly of interest to women and delicate boys, who were obviously ignorant as to what constituted a 'proper' motorcycle. Douglas at Bristol began making Vespas in 1950 for one ominous reason only; the company was bankrupt.

The typical British response can be summed up in one phrase: too little, too late. Prototype scooters such as the Oscar, a bulbous glass-fibre contraption, and the Harper, made by a small aircraft company in Exeter, aroused interest in the early 1950s but never went into volume production. At the 1955 Motor Cycle Show the giant BSA group unveiled their design study, the Beeza, which had an old-fashioned, side-valve, 175cc four-stroke engine set in a complex series of alloy fabricated sections. Again, though despite a good public response,

it was never put into production.

The British scooters which were produced in quantity from the late Fifties onwards were usually powered by so-called 'proprietary' engines, often made by Villiers. Such 150- to 250cc-sized single or twin-cylinder two-strokes could be found in lawnmowers, primitive bubble cars and a host of poorly assembled British motorcycles of the time. Scooters such as the Dayton Albatross (possibly the most honestly named British scooter

ever made), the DKW Dove of 1957, the Phoenix, the Panther Princess built in Cleckheaton, the Bond P3 and P4, Sun Geni and 250cc Sunwasp all used Villiers power. There was just one problem with the Villiers two-stroke engine; it was unreliable rubbish.

To compound this basic error, British scooter construction was usually achieved by lashing the engine into a Heath Robinson-style lattice of steel tubes, brackets and hastily welded plates, then covering

ABOVE: THE DAYTON ALBATROSS WAS ONE OF MANY
UNDERDEVELOPED BRITISH SCOOTERS

LEFT: THE BSA SUNBEAM WAS MARKETED AS LUXURY TRANSPORT

the mess with steel panels.

Bizarre solutions to limited space made British scooters challenging to ride; for example, the DKW Dove (and the Excelsior Monarch, which shared the same chassis) had a large fuel tank located in the front body section, placing lots of weight right above the front wheel. Edward Turner, legendary designer of the Triumph Speed Twin, came up with a scooter called the Triumph Tigress

(also the BSA Sunbeam) which had two tiny inspection holes set in the side panels to enable engine maintenance. If you were a double-jointed gibbon, this arrangement was fine.

Turner's scooter wasn't actually a bad effort: rather handsome in its looks, too. But after beginning the project in 1955, it took the BSA-Triumph group another three years to get a model on show

THE BSA BEEZA DESIGN STUDY AT THE 1955 UK MOTORCYCLE SHOW

ENIGMATIC VARIATIONS: LAMBRETTAS WERE ALWAYS POPULAR IN ENGLAND: AN EARLY 1950S MODEL WITH A ROOF AND AN RAC SIDECAR PATROL

to the public and a further two years to make the scooters in any volume.

The peak in 1959 for moped and scooter sales in the UK — some 180,000 units — concentrated minds in the boardrooms of Britain, but by then it was too late. Scooters like the Triumph Tina and the Velocette Viceroy, launched in the early Sixties just as the market rapidly went into decline, were the humiliating last

TRIUMPH CHANGED THEIR SALES PITCH FROM THE MAN-WITH-A-PIPE WHEN THEY PRODUCED SCOOTERS

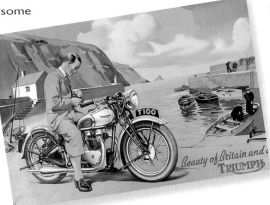

Beauty of Britain and TRIUMPH

scene in a long-running British farce. One British motorcycle dealer of the early Sixties, Ted Williams from Wrexham, North Wales, recalled the 99cc Tina:

'Everything that could go possibly wrong with it did, pretty much from when I bought it brand-new for my wife Dot. In fact that bloody Tina probably brought us closer to divorce than anything else in 40 years of married life.'

The Sun Almost Rises

The Italians had also had a lucky escape in the 1950s – or a temporary reprieve, as it turned out – from another competitor; Japan.

Again, here was a country which had suffered terrible war damage, then substantial American investment in the late 1940s. The Americans had examples of their Cushman military scooters in Japan and they also forced the main Japanese wartime ordnance supplier to split into 12 separate companies, none of which would be permitted to produce arms.

In 1946 the Fuji-Subaru company launched their scooter, the Rabbit, which used a tubular frame and rear-mounted engine like the Lambretta. It was also very similar to the Cushman in terms of its boxy styling. The makers of the famous Zero fighter plane, Mitsubishi, produced the Silver Pigeon a year later.

MOSTLY PLASTIC: THE RABBIT STAYED IN PRODUCTION IN JAPAN FOR OVER 20 YEARS

Both were models were basic machines, using the 100cc-sized two-stroke power units available at the time, most of which had been developed in the war

For the Italian, French, German and British scooter-makers, the fact that almost all Japan's two-wheeled output in the 1950s was designed solely for their seemingly insatiable home market was a lucky break. The pace of technical change and product improvement was incredibly fast, as intense competition whittled down the motorcycle manufacturers to less than 30 by 1960. Like Mitsubishi, Fuji-Subaru stopped making the Rabbit and concentrated on cars instead. Only one Japanese motorcycle manufacturer in the late 1950s dreamed of exporting a cheap 50cc runabout vehicle in massive numbers to Europe; Honda.

Topper Comes A Cropper

Not all of **Vespa and Lambretta's competitors got the scooter** idea right, of course. But if you thought some of the British scooters were poor, take a look at what the biggest bike maker in America came up with: the Harley-Davidson Topper.

Like Britain, the USA turned down the blueprints for the VW Beetle car as part of the war reparations deal. Instead, both allies grabbed the German DKW 125cc two-stroke engine, which must have seemed much more useful at the time. The Americans ultimately provided the cash which created the Vespa, Lambretta, Fuji Rabbit and many more, but when it came to designing their own scooter, Americans hadn't a clue.

In fact, they went over to Italy in the late 1950s and bought 50 per cent of Aermacchi – the former Schneider Trophy seaplane manufacturers on the shores of Lake Varese. Aermacchi were already building motorcycles – quite well, in fact – so making a scooter at Varese must have seemed like a guaranteed money-spinning idea.

The Topper was yet another variant of the old Cushman wartime scooter. Underneath its boxy bodywork it had the 165cc version of the original DKW engine, which was laid flat at the back ... under possibly the most hideously ugly vehicle ever made in Italy. A chain-driven pulley arrangement provided automatic transmission and the top speed was barely 40mph. that was a good thing, because the Topper had no front brake fitted.

THE HARLEY NO ONE LIKES TO TALK ABOUT: THE CURIOUS TOPPER

The Topper, like many British scooters, was launched too late – in 1960, when the scooter boom was over. Produced for five years by Aermacchi, until appalingly low sales put the thing out of its misery, the Harley-Davidson scooter was a poorly-assembled, pig-ugly, wheezing insult to anyone who thought that 'American-made' meant it was bigger and better.

③ The Modern World

Vespa and Lambretta entered the 1960s with the firm idea of cleaning up financially in the world of low-cost, mass-market transport. Movie stars were still very much on the payroll and advertising in 'youth' magazines in Europe brought new converts every weekend. In fact the scooter was quickly being adopted as the preferred transport of a London-based cult movement in the early Sixties — a group of young men called Mods.

ABOVE AND LEFT: **THE MODS DECORATED THEIR SCOOTERS WITH PENNANTS, BADGES AND MIRRORS TO CELEBRATE THEIR REBELLION IN STYLE**

MANY A MOD WOULD START THEIR SCOOTERING CAREER ON A SECOND-HAND EXAMPLE FROM THE 1950S

Mod was a reaction by a new generation of teenagers to the greasy quiffs, leather jackets, Edwardian suits and raucous R 'n' B-inspired music of the original Fifties rock-and-rollers. Their suits were tighter, Italian-style, with slim lapels and short jackets. Mod hairstyles were shorter, too, and the soundtrack to their weekend posing rituals was called Soul, drawing inspiration from the industrial northern cities of America. It was a sharper look altogether, and very much at the leading edge of pop culture and youth fashion between 1962 and 1966.

Lambretta had hit the nail on the head and beaten the pack in 1962 with their TV175 Slimstyle model, which became a favourite scooter with the Mods. Essentially a re-worked Li150 in the engine department, the Slimstyle broke new ground with its bodywork, an entirely fresh design which set the tone for the

classic Sixties scooter. Narrower legshields, footboards and a flat section on each side panel beneath the rider gave the whole package a new, modern look. This was a scooter which matched your latest tailored suit and Italian shoes, a cool way to get around town, a crucial accessory in becoming a 'face'.

Roadtests of the time praised the TV175 for its speed: it could hit 65mph, which was as fast as most lightweight British motorcycles could manage. It also had a front disc brake which, although little better than a twin-leading shoe drum, was a genuine first in the two-wheeled world, some seven years ahead of the Honda CB750. Again, this was a scooter manufacturer taking technology from the aero industry, where disc brakes had been developed to stop bombers from over-shooting runways upon landing.

The United Kingdom was Lambretta's most important European market at

THE LAMBRETTA GT200, ONE OF THE MOST POPULAR 'SLIMSTYLE' SCOOTERS

NEED TO BE SEEN: BRITISH MODS OUT AND ABOUT. ABOVE: IN BRIXTON, LONDON
BELOW: ON THE RUN: MODS IN CLACTON IN 1964

this time and the British importers were no doubt delighted with the Slimstyle range and the 1963 GT200 – the fastest Lammy yet, which they had specifically requested the factory to produce.

The GT200 (also called the TV200) was a real looker, too, available in white with four colour options. Right to the end of the Sixties, Lambretta had ads with cool cartoon heroes boasting of 'SX appeal' in their figure-hugging suits. This was important in building up the Lambretta as the

ABOVE: SCOOTING THROUGH CLACTON IN 1964

LAMBRETTA WAS STILL SELLING STRONGLY IN 1964

young person's scooter; the faster, more fashionable scooter to own.

Not everything Lambretta did looks so trendy now, of course. There was even a special edition Lambretta model called the Pacemaker, named after pop stars Gerry and the Pacemakers, who were a popular beat combo from Liverpool back in 1963. Gerry and the boys appeared in the advertising campaign for the model. It didn't date well, but you'll never scoot alone, Gerry.

Turn On The style

Vespa weren't slow to compete in this ultra-trendy market, of course. Their 1961 Sportique 150 was available in a special "Bahama Gold" paint job, or a version with chromium-plated panels. Features such as a parking light, steering lock, dual seat etc. were all fitted as standard.

The following year saw the launch of perhaps the classic Sixties Vespa, the GS160, which looked the absolute minimalist business in its white livery. It also had increased acceleration and a top speed hovering around the 60mph mark in fourth gear. The Mark Two version, which came out just a year later, in 1963, got a good-looking, built-in front luggage compartment too — ideal for stashing your essential gear and taking a trip down to the coast in the summer.

THE VESPA SPORTIQUE 150: ANY MOD'S DREAM
MACHINE AND STILL POPULAR TODAY

ON THE SET: THE MOVIE QUADROPHENIA CAUSED A REVIVAL OF SCOOTER POPULARITY IN THE LATE 1970S. ABOVE: STING; BELOW RIGHT: PHIL DANIELS

DAVE CLA

Pop Goes The Scooter

Ironically, despite all the hype, the Mod movement was almost a swansong for scooters in many European countries. By making the vehicle incredibly fashionable, the Mods condemned the scooter to go out of style at some point in the Sixties, which came just after the 1967 'Summer of Love'. Suits were definitely not on the hippie agenda and the £12,000 which The Small Faces were rumoured to spend on clothes in 1966 was a last gasp for consumerism for a few years.

In general, scooter sales had been in decline across most of modern Europe for the whole of the Sixties, with a sudden collapse from the incredible peaks of the late 1950s. In Britain, for example, the scooter market shrank by around 75 per cent between 1959 and 1963, dropping to somewhere around 35,000 new units. France, Germany, Austria and the Low Countries all experienced similar reversals. In warmer climates like Spain and Italy the drop wasn't so sudden, but the decline was an inexorable, unstoppable process.

There were many factors involved, but the main reason was simple; people had more money, so they bought a car. It was the vehicle most people, especially those with children, aspired to owning. Even back in the 1950s that desire was

SCOOTER SALES HAD BEEN IN DECLINE ACROSS MOST OF MODERN EUROPE FOR THE WHOLE OF THE SIXTIES

COOL FOR CATS: SIXTIES POP STARS LIKE DAVE CLARK (FAR LEFT) AND GERRY & THE PACEMAKERS (LEFT) GOT IN ON THE SCOOTER BOOM

there, but the average wage-earner simply couldn't afford a car until the Sixties.

In Britain, the violent clashes between Mods and Rockers at beach resorts during the mid-Sixties didn't help to promote scooter sales either. Although the fighting that took place at Clacton, Margate and Brighton during 1964–66 seems almost tame by today's standards, it was seized on by the two main tabloid newspapers

MODFATHER PAUL WELLER CHOOSES A PAIR OF LAMBRETTAS FOR *STANLEY ROAD*

of the time, the *Daily Mirror* and *Daily Sketch* (later *The Sun*), as a convenient way of boosting their circulations in the 'silly season' but traditionally quiet summer months. The situation even led to questions being asked in Parliament. 'Ordinary' people began quietly trading in their basic Vespas, Lambrettas and other scooters for something which didn't attract the wrong sort of attention.

Hello Mini, Goodbye Lambretta

But with supreme irony, the greatest threat to Innocenti Lambretta came from within their own plant; the Mini.

Designed by Sir Alec Issigonis, the 1959 BMC Mini was one of the icons of the Sixties, a car loved by millions of people regardless of race, class or gender. It was also one of the cheapest cars on the market thanks to its simple, seam-welded, pressed-steel construction. The British Motor Corporation took effective control of the Innocenti company in 1965, as they expanded upon strong UK market car sales. Although Innocenti had a lucrative business selling lightweight three-wheeler delivery vehicles, BMC decided to manufacture the Mini in Italy, to cash in on the car's Continental chic.

New Lambretta scooters were still appearing throughout the late Sixties as Innocenti became more concerned with car production. Arguably one of the best scooters of the time appeared in 1966, the Lambretta SX200.

SUN, SEA AND SCOOTER: BUT IT WAS THE BEGINNING OF THE END FOR LAMBRETTA

**THE GP200
ELECTRONICA
MODEL LAMBRETTA**

In 1968, Italian styling guru Bertone designed the hip 'ink-blot' GP range which, according to the legend, sported the ink splash on the legshield where the great man had accidentally marked his drawing-board. The Bertone models entered the market in 1969.

Perhaps the last Lammy was the best Innocenti-built scooter of them all; the GP200 Electronic of 1970. With no fiddly ignition points to keep setting, it was inherently more reliable and decently quick too. The Lui/Vega 50cc scooter of the same year was also popular on the Continent. Unfortunately the British Motor Corporation were only interested in producing as many cars as they could: they saw scooters as old-fashioned and barely profitable. In the boardroom, they thought the future was in four wheels, not two.

Innocenti also caught a nasty dose of the British disease — lightning strikes by the workforce — which helped seal its fate. BMC closed Innocenti in 1972, just a year before the OPEC oil cartel quadrupled the cost of a barrel of crude and sent petrol pump prices skywards. By then, the Indian government had bought the entire tooling, jigs and production equipment for the GP200 from Innocenti's plant. The last Lambretta is still available as an import from India today, called the Bajaj Chetak. Another variation on the GP200 continued to be made at the Servetta factory in Spain for most of the 1970s, but the market in Europe all but disappeared for Lambretta scooters without large-scale factory support. Spares supply and quality control were poor. It seemed nobody cared that the Lammy was dead, except the old Mods.

THE LAMBRETTA GP200 'INK BLOT' MODEL, DESIGNED BY BERTONE OF ITALY

Avanti Piaggio

**SGR ALBERTO
AGNELLI ON A
PIAGGIO SFERA**

Piaggio survived this sea-change in consumer habits by constantly seeking out new markets in the developing world for their ubiquitous Vespa. Like Innocenti, they began exporting scooters from their earliest days, but more importantly, Piaggio began producing scooters in factories built abroad to meet sudden upswings in local demand, as individual countries experienced the same process of increasing prosperity as Europe had enjoyed in the 1950s. Labour was cheaper and less strike-prone than in Italy, and partnerships with overseas vehicle producers shared the initial production start-up costs.

**THE 'NEW LINE'
VESPA SCOOTER
OF 1978**

La Bella Antonella

Yet perhaps the most significant factor in Piaggio's long-term survival, and conversely in Innocenti's doom, was the marriage which took place in 1959 between Antonella Piaggio (Enrico's daughter) and Umberto Agnelli – the heir to the Fiat empire. Suddenly, two Italian powerhouses of industry became one. From then on, the Vespa and its related models were more or less guaranteed a future.

So Piaggio steadily produced variations on the tried and tested Sixties Vespa through the 1970s and most of the Eighties – for a worldwide customer base, not just a European one. Piaggio's Indonesian factory, opened in 1970, was their first overseas manufacturing facility.

Lambretta's exit left the European scooter market, albeit much reduced,

THE SCOOTER IS STILL THE WORKHORSE OF THE WORLD FOR MILLIONS
OF PEOPLE IN DEVELOPING NATIONS

BELOW RIGHT: CHETAK OF INDIA PRODUCE SCOOTERS USING OLD VESPA TOOLS

pretty much a monopoly for them. In Spain, the Moto Vespe facility outpaced Servetta, whilst Pontedera kept demand satisfied in Italy, France, Germany and much of Western Europe. The Rally 180 and 200 Electronic were popular, as was the 50cc three-speed moped/scooter, which featured pedals if local laws specified it. The European fuel crises of the 1970s boosted demand for both the 50cc Vespa scooter and a basic step-through moped called the Ciao, as car drivers across Europe struggled with sudden pump price increases, shortages and at one stage even ration-books.

Such steady demand and a lack of competition from 1970 onwards made Piaggio look a little stale. There were no fundamental attempts by Piaggio to update their Vespa range, in fact, until almost the close of the decade, with the introduction of the New Line range in 1978.

The 'New Line' Vespa makeover in 1978 was essentially a

THE VESPA PX RANGE HAS BEEN POPULAR FOR TWO DECADES. BLUR'S DAMON ALBARN OWNS ONE

new skin on some old scooters, giving Piaggios a boxy, angular look that fitted in more with the automotive fashions of the decade. To some eyes, the square tail-light cluster looked as if it might have come straight from a Fiat Mirafiori 132 car.

This new body shape had a best-seller in the shape of the long-lived PX range: in fact the PX celebrated 20 years of production in 1997. The PX and its old-school Mod-style brother, the T5, are still in production today and are much sought-after by true scooter *cognoscenti*. Modfather of Britpop Mr Paul Weller has a PX model, as does Blur's singer Damon Albarn and Steve Craddock from Ocean Colour Scene. The 'New Line' range were the last 'real' Vespas for many scooterists — simple, compact machines that stretched right back stylistically to d'Ascanio, Hepburn and Fellini — a little echo of a vanished Italy.

OCEAN COLOUR SCENE GUITARIST STEVE CRADDOCK
IS ANOTHER VESPA PX FAN

4 Now Is The Time

In most European countries the 1990s have seen an incredible revival in the popularity of scootering. As in the 1950s, people from all ages and social classes have takenma to machines with two wheels and enclosed engines once more, but this time for fun, fashion and getting around gridlocked cities. But, differing from the original scootering ideals, two fundamental influences now drive European scooter design and manufacture; style and technology.

ABOVE: **MOD STYLES ARE POPULAR AGAIN**

LEFT: **THE BAND MEMBERS OF OASIS EACH OWN AN ITALJET VELOCIFERO 50**

ITALJET ALSO MAKE THE FUNKY LOOKING F50 AND F125 MODELS, WITH THE 125CC MACHINE (ABOVE) BEING THE ONLY TWIN CYLINDER ENGINE SCOOTER ON THE MARKET TODAY

The most important of the two is probably technology, since the sheer convenience and ease of use of today's rev 'n' go city scooters have convinced thousands of sceptical car-owners to give it a try. But the roots of the luxurious, gadget-packed 1990s commuter scooter lie in the previous decade.

In 1983 Honda launched a model that influenced an entire generation of scooter designers from Tokyo to Turin: the CH125 Spacy.

In essence, the Spacy was little more than a dash of radical, angular Eighties styling grafted on to their new Vision 50–80cc shopper scooters, a bigger-than-usual 125cc engine, plus the added gimmick of a built-in foot-level heater to lure unsuspecting car drivers. How a heater on an open scooter could make any real difference to the air temperature around your shoes is a debatable point. Yet Honda were being, as

ABOVE: **BOY TOY: THE HONDA X8R**

ABOVE: **THE HONDA SPACY 125.** BELOW: **THE TRICK ITALJET F50**

ever, highly innovative with the scooter concept.

The Spacy was a bold move, not only for its styling, which was up to the minute for 1983, but because by choosing a 125cc-class, longer-bodied scooter Honda were looking ahead, to a time when car drivers en masse would finally be tempted out of their tin boxes in the traffic-choked cities of the developed world.

A 125cc engine was small enough to sip fuel at about 100mpg, but also large enough to accelerate from standstill to 50mph without too much effort. Even in the Eighties, 50cc mopeds and scooters simply got left behind at traffic lights by the average saloon, so Honda were making the scooter commuter capable of cutting through the traffic whenever a gap opened up — a mixture of speed and style to fit the pace of urban living.

Three Wheels On My Wagon

1983 also saw Honda's attempt to revive the BSA/Ariel Pixie three-wheeled, moped/scooter concept, dubbed the Stream. This had a 50cc two-stroke engine in a scooter body which had a hinged frame under the rider, so that the luggage box on the back stayed upright on its twin-wheel axle while the forward section tilted like a conventional motorbike. The three-wheeled concept never really caught on outside Japan, though Honda still make a three-wheeler called the Canopy today. Underneath the new plastic body-work and the roof – yes, a scooter with a roof – the Canopy is basically a modernized Stream. It's popular with fast-food delivery firms all over the world.

The Spacy was a reasonable success in Europe. It was particularly popular in Italy, where style always counted for more than technology when it came to scooters. At that stage, Lambretta had been out of production for a decade and Vespa models were beginning to look dated to the trendier urbanites. The Vespa PX range, which was launched in the same year as the Spacy and Stream Hondas, is considered a design classic now but back then, to commuters looking for transport with style and ease of use, the Honda scooters somehow seemed more modern, more appealing.

THE YAMAHA BWS, ALSO CALLED B-WIZZ AND JOG IN SOME MARKETS

In a move which signalled a clear intention to sell large numbers of small-capacity, two-wheeled vehicles in Europe, Honda bought factories in Italy and Spain during the early 1980s too.

Other manufacturers gradually followed Honda's lead throughout the Eighties. Yamaha decided not to bring their Tracy scooter to Europe, which not only sounded but also looked similar to

THE FUTURISTIC THREE-WHEELED HONDA STREAM

the Spacy. However, the cheekily styled 50cc and 80cc-sized BWs (also called Jog and B-Wizz) were very popular, particularly with women riders. It too looked a little bit different from the traditional scooter shape.

Yamaha also purchased Motobecane (MBK) of France and the Minarelli engine company in Italy. The Japanese were setting up shop in Piaggio's back yard.

Relax In the Armchair Scooter

In 1988 Honda gave the Spacy even more futuristic looks and squeezed in a 250cc four-stroke engine unit, making room by stretching the chassis. The scooter which established a new class — super scooters — had arrived. Called the CN250, Spazio, Fusion or Helix, depending on which part of the world you lived in, its car-inspired dashboard, floor mats, body panels, stepped dual seat and long 'droop snoot' nose section made every other scooter on the market look outdated. The future was right here, right now.

But not many people were ready for the future. Although the CN250 was a patchy success it was nevertheless very expensive for a scooter, retailing at around £3,000. From 1988–90, the UK market only took 551 CN250 models. The new, feet-forward scooter appealed to those with money to spare who were free-thinking too — the Cosworth-series car engine designer Keith Duckworth bought one.

It took until the turn of the 1990s for the other manufacturers to realize that there was a vast potential market for bigger, more luxurious and faster scooters. Piaggio finally responded to Honda with the 125cc Hexagon in 1991. With an almost identical body profile, right down to the stepped seating, it was easy to see where Pontedera's designers had been looking for inspiration. Still using a 125cc two-stroke engine, the Hexagon was a good try by Piaggio, but nothing radical set it apart from the Honda CN250, and with half the engine capacity it was also slightly slower.

**THE PIAGGIO
HEXAGON 125**

THE HONDA CN250

In one respect, Piaggio didn't have to beat Honda at producing a super scooter for the final decade of the 20th century. The Italian giant had racked up an astonishing 15 million scooter sales worldwide by the early 1990s and was in partnership with, or had acquired a major shareholding in, many smaller companies active in two-wheeler production. Piaggio were busy selling hundreds of thousands of units in rapidly developing markets in the Far Eastern 'tiger' economies of the late 1980s. People

**FOR THE YOUTH:
THE PIAGGIO
SKIPPER 125**

there wanted a scooter which cost very little to run, so a mobile-phone socket wasn't a priority.

In addition, Piaggio had a run-away success on its hands across Europe in the early 1990s in the shape of the Skipper 125 and 150 models. Developed from the ground-breaking Sfera machine of the mid-1980s – the first modern-day Piaggio – the Skipper was a versatile, well-equipped scooter for anyone who wanted easy urban travel. Promoted with sponsorship on the MTV Europe

ABOVE: THE SFERA 125 WAS PIAGGIO'S FIRST FOUR STROKE
BELOW: THE YAMAHA MAJESTY 250 AND SUZUKI BURGMAN 250 SUPER-SCOOTERS

satellite TV channel, the Skipper was Europe's best-selling scooter for two years running, capturing many thousands of new teenage customers for scootering in general.

It was left up to the Japanese to stimulate the feet-forward, large-capacity scooter market in Europe in the mid-1990s, targeting an older, more affluent client base.

Yamaha launched their YP250 Majesty in 1996 which had a four-stroke, water-cooled, single-cylinder engine driving through an automatic three-speed gearbox, giving it a top speed of 75mph. Lots of luggage space, disc front braking and a remarkably restrained body style gave the Majesty a distinctive look. In a word it

DETAILS OF THE TRENDY SFERA 125

was classy: so classy, in fact, that it went on to become the best-selling two-wheeled vehicle in Italy during 1997.

Suzuki followed suit with their Burgman in 1997, available first in a 250cc size, then the following year launched as a 100mph, 385cc-engined machine. The Burgman took the super scooter to the edge of its design limitations. With a substantial steel tubular frame, plush seating including passenger backrest, linked disc braking front and rear and 13-inch wheels, the Burgman is a borderline touring motorcycle – a pocket Pan-European 800.

As the domestic demand in countries like Taiwan levelled off, some manufacturers, such as PGO, Chunlun, Her Chee, Kymco and

Sanyang all started bringing their two-wheelers to Europe, some of which were already in the super scooter class. The Kymco Dink 125, for example, achieved instant success in Italy with its child-like styling. Yamaha brought their Fly One, built at their Taiwan facility, to mainland Europe. Sanyang (known by the name of `SYM in the UK), who produce over 2,000 scooters per day in Taiwan and are part-owned by Honda, have a prototype electric executive scooter called the Aspire under development.

Italian companies such as Aprilia, with their long-wheelbase, four-stroke-powered Leonardo appearing in 125cc and 150cc guise during 1996, and Malaguti with their Madison of 1998 (which uses the Yamaha Majesty 250cc engine) proved that the home team weren't totally oblivious to the current design trends either.

ABOVE: THE PEUGEOT ELYSEO 125

BELOW: THE BENELLI 491

The giant French automotive group Peugeot also launched their Elyseo 125 in 1998, with a new-generation, liquid-cooled, 125cc four-stroke engine inside it: an engine and transmission unit which they will be hoping to sell to many other distributors and manufacturers worldwide.

The next 10 years are predicted to see a rise in most European nations' road traffic volumes of between 40 and 70 per cent, depending on which survey you believe. What is certain is that governments are going to find ways of taxing motorists harshly to relieve traffic congestion without building expensive new roads. Tolls, electronic swipe cards or even scannable barcodes on vehicles are all methods being seriously considered by European governments to relieve traffic jams. The era of the large scooter as the second car could be just around the corner.

ABOVE: THE HONDA FORESIGHT 250

BELOW LEFT: THE BIG WHEEL APRILIA SCARABEO AND THE MALAGUTI MADISON 150

From Metro To Retro

As the 1990s progressed, the 'retro' look became more prevalent in all forms of two-wheeled transport, from a 1,340cc Harley-Davidson Bad Boy to a Honda Monkey Bike. However, the credit for successfully defining what a retro scooter should look like during the Nineties goes to a relatively small Italian company, Italjet, with their stunning 1993 creation, the Velocifero.

Sitting on tiny eight-inch wheels, with an automatic 50cc engine moving its pressed-steel section chassis, the Velocifero is Italjet's modern-day homage to Corradino d'Ascanio's original Vespa. Leading London fashion designer Patrick Cox was commissioned to create a limited edition model, which was only available in a retro Mod black and white paint scheme with a leopardskin saddle cover. Nice.

The Velocifero was a runaway success, with pop stars, film and TV celebrities queuing up to buy it. Oasis stars Noel and Liam Gallagher bought one apiece and Robbie Williams occasionally joined Liam for a trip down to Tesco. REM singer Michael Stipe reportedly owns five Velos — perhaps shopping for scooters helps cheer him up? Patrick Cox once stated that he wanted to make his special edition Velocifero:

'the last word in urban chic'

COUTURE SCOOTER: THE PATRICK COX VELOCIFERO

ABOVE: THE 16 INCH WHEEL ITALJET TORPEDO
BELOW: STAND OUT ON A VELOCIFERO

**POP STARS TAKE A
SCOOTER TRIP**

During the summer of 1997, it was without doubt the scooter to be seen on around London, although like most fashion icons it seems to be slipping out of favour as the century closes. The latest retro look is a bizarre trend from Southern Europe called 'Big Wheel' scooters. Starting with the popular craze in Spain around 1994 for the 16-inch Honda Scoopy (also called the Sky 50) moped/scooter, other firms have exploited the fad. Piaggio's Liberty and Peperino (a tribute by Piaggio to d'Ascanio's original design) models, Moto Guzzi's Galetto concept scooter, Benelli's Pepe, the Aprilia Scarabeo, Yamaha's Why 50 and more all demonstrate how the manufacturers of the 1990s are determined to leave no gap in the scooter market. This fusion of retro and modern styling details has taken Nineties scooters beyond commuting to the level of designer tag couture. Trainers, watch, sunglasses and scooter – a new uniform for city life.

London-based TV presenter, radio broadcaster and former sarong-wearing celebrity-about-town Jonathan Ross owns an Italjet Velocifero, which is of course a custom-painted Patrick Cox edition. In an issue of *Petrolhead* magazine, Jonathan tried to define the appeal of modern urban scooter riding:

'Riding across Waterloo Bridge on a clear day, not much traffic about, Big Ben on the right, St. Paul's on the left and lots of riverboats below … it's all you need for the perfect Zen moment'

**SIMON AND
YASMIN LE BON
ON A PIAGGIO ET2**

'MODERN' MODS: A SCOOTER RUN, 1990S STYLE (LEFT); MERC OF LONDON
DRAW INSPIRATION FROM THE SUEDEHEAD/SCOOTERBOY
LOOK OF THE EARLY 1970S

Wacky Racers

Tuning an engine for more speed is probably Italy's second-oldest profession. Kids of all ages love to race and the scooter has been tinkered with since its invention. But in the early 1990s the factories themselves started to get in on the act and a new generation of hi-tech 'pocket rocket' scooters appeared.

First up to the traffic lights was the Williams Italjet Formula 50. This was developed from the sort of crazily fast, disc-braked, alloy-wheeled paddock bikes with which Formula One car racing teams were busily filling their pitlane garages in the Eighties. The F50 obviously appealed to speed-crazy characters of all ages, but it wasn't just a special paint job and a hotter spark plug. It was a beautifully engineered machine in its own right, which in a short time led Italjet to create the superb twin-cylinder-engined F125. This featured powerful disc brakes, hub-centre steering, twin exhausts exiting on the right-hand side of the machine and ultra-sharp styling.

The Spanish-made Derbi Predator 100, the Malaguti F12 Phantom, Aprilia

REAL RACER: THE WILLIAMS SPECIAL EDITION ITALJET F50 SCOOTER

Stealth SR50, Honda X8-R, Peugeot Speedfight 100, Gilera Runner 180, Piaggio Typhoon 125, Benelli 491 and many more are all in the same vein. All have front disc brakes, trick suspension, which is usually in the shape of upside-down telescopic forks and a pair of gas-activated shocks at the back, and pointy-nosed styling. The new manufacturers from Taiwan have also been quick to jump on this band-wagon, with the models like the Kymco Cobra, PGO PMX 90 and SYM Jet 100 all following the pattern.

They're all scoots for popping a wheelie on, standing it on its nose at junctions, sliding sideways in the wet. Boys' toys: extreme machines for the Pepsi Max generation who want to wipe out on the Paris Péripherique before they get old. The irony is that these race-replica scooters are perhaps the safest you can buy,

since their handling, braking and performance make dodging psychotic taxi drivers, mobile-phone-yapping pedestrians and other traffic hazards a cinch.

Italjet arguably still lead the pack of wacky racers, with their strangely beautiful Dragster. Appearing in 1997, this 49cc machine features a trellis frame like a Ducati, hub-centre steering like a Bimota Tesi and a horizontally set shock absorber à la Buell. But it isn't a motorbike. It is — well, no one is quite sure what it is actually, but everyone agrees that the Dragster is utterly different: a scooter designed by an alien civilization.

In 1998 Italjet announced that the Dragster would be getting the Gilera 180cc engine (actually manufactured by Piaggio and fitted to their Hexagon too) in its Spartan skeleton frame, making this perhaps the most exotic, and possibly expensive, scooter on the market — kind of Pepsi Max meets Mad Max.

ABOVE: **MALAGUTI PHANTOM**
BELOW: **F1 BOYS JUST WANNA HAVE FUN**

ABOVE: THE ITALJET DRAGSTER IS POSSIBLY THE CRAZIEST
LOOKING SCOOTER IN THE WORLD.
BELOW: ITALJET'S DESIGNERS DARE TO BE DIFFERENT

DRAGSTER HAS MORE RADICAL CHASSIS TECHNOLOGY THAN MANY £15,000 MOTORCYCLES

⑤ 21st Century Toys

Although big motorcycles have more speed, kudos and, some would say, style than the humble little scooter, the overwhelming majority of two-wheeled vehicles in the world are lightweight commuters, with engines under 125cc. Many of these are scooters, and the new generation of them are emerging more stylish, safe and practical than ever before. In the 50 years that scooters have been mass-produced around the world, they have changed an unbelievable amount.

ABOVE: **THE SPICESONIC SCOOTER**

LEFT: **THE PEPERINO IS PIAGGIO'S 1990S HOMAGE TO D'ASCANIO'S ORIGINAL PAPARINO PROTOTYPE BUT IS UNLIKELY TO GO INTO PRODUCTION**

The scooter is still a perfect transport solution for millions of daily
users. The global statistics are staggering in their scale and soon make anyone in Europe realize that we enjoy a diverse collection of fashionable bikes and
scooters on the back of huge utility machine sales worldwide.

World motorcycle production currently stands at around 17 million units
per year, mostly utility machines under 100cc, which is roughly what Piaggio
have produced in total since 1946. Most mopeds and scooters are made in Asia,
with mainland China leading the way.

In China, two-wheeler production has rocketed since the 1980s, with annual new sales in 1997 of around 6.5 million units. To put it into perspective, the
entire sale of motorcycles, mopeds and scooters in the EU during 1997 was
around a tenth of that, at some 620,000 vehicles.

Honda, who committed themselves to a multi-million-dollar investment

**THE GILERA RUNNER
IS AVAILABLE IN
180CC SIZE, CAPABLE
OF 75MPH, WHERE
LEGAL OF COURSE**

with China's largest motor-cycle producer, Jialing, in the 1980s, also have factories in Thailand, Taiwan, Malaysia and other Asian countries. In Vietnam, for example, Honda's subsidiary plant pro-duces over 30,000 mopeds and scooters per month; or, to put it another way, more than the entire annual new motorcycle market for the Netherlands. Yamaha, Suzuki and Kawasaki have all made similar large-scale investments in China.

Without selling several hundred

TOP: **PIAGGIO'S LIBERTY 125.** ABOVE: **GILERA RUNNER 180**

thousand two-stroke com-muters a year, enthusiasts would probably never have seen an RC45, Yamaha R1 or 180mph Suzuki Hayabusa from the Japanese giants.

If you want a new Lambretta GP200, contact Bajaj of India, who make around half a mil-lion of them each year and export them around the world. Should you fancy something slightly more modern, then Piaggio's LML partner in India are man-ufacturing approximately 300,000 Vespa scooters every year.

Plug In And Play

As cities around the world grind to a halt, while a million car drivers a day seemingly compete for the same 37 parking spaces, the scooter – in Europe at least – looks set to be reborn; as an electrical appliance.

Since the late 1980s various manufacturers and madcap inventors such as Sir Clive Sinclair have been searching for a viable electric transport vehicle for solo use. Recent advances in battery cell technology mean that speeds can now hit 40mph, with a similar range in miles between recharging sessions – ideal for commuting.

Piaggio have already gone halfway to this mode of transport with their Zip & Zip model, launched in 1995. This hybrid offers the rider the choice between a small, petrol-sipping 50cc engine and an electric power source, depending on the local laws. Already some mainland European inner-cities are restricting access to petrol-engined vehicles, whilst offering unlimited travel to electric-aided vehicles, all geared towards encouraging increased 'green' vehicle usage. It's a concept which looks set to grow, with a little bit of the petrol engine's energy recharging the batteries, minimizing mains-recharging time. Several car-makers are also well advanced along the hybrid engine route.

But all the major scooter/motorcycle manufacturers look likely to launch fully electric scooters over the next few years, as governments are bringing in new 'greener' transport laws. Peugeot are there already, with the Scoot'elec model, featuring a top speed of just 28mph. That isn't fast enough to keep up

THE APPLIANCE OF SCIENCE: THE PEUGOET 'ELEC

with traffic in most cities, but the scooter is a good-looking, well thought-out concept in every other respect.

The bottom line with electric scooters is that they are ahead of their economic 'window'. Oil is too cheap and plentiful at present for

FUTURE SCOOTERS WILL BE SMOOTH, SILENT TYPES

manufacturers to tool up production lines for such minority-interest vehicles. However, when oil becomes black gold once again, which is inevitable with something finite, then the era of the electric bike will be here to stay, like it or not.

German Expressionism

One German automotive conglomerate has been researching solutions to urban gridlock for years. In fact, BMW revived an idea from the 1950s and gave it a clever update; the two-wheeled car. Their C1 scooter prototype broke cover back in 1992 and has been in development ever since, with a launch planned in the year 2000 for this revolutionary city scooter.

Essentially an egg-shaped, twin-spar alloy hoop on wheels, the C1 has been designed to be the safest two-wheeler in the world. On BMW's website, the sceptical car driver can watch video footage of C1 machines being crash-tested in scary slow motion. But the scooter's safety cage — and the rider inside — stay intact. The real genius of the design is that no helmet is necessary to prevent fatal injury, as there are foam-section side impact protectors and a headrest to cushion the rider's head. Indeed, BMW state that wearing a helmet might actually increase the risk of serious whiplash injury.

The C1 will initially be available in five different models, with features such as a mobile-phone-holder, roof, windscreen wiper and two safety harnesses for the rider as standard. Options will include things such as a CD player, satellite navigation and anti-lock braking system. An electric motor version is also planned.

If BMW can persuade the TUV organization, who act as arbiters on transport safety regulations in Germany, that the C1 can have an exemption from the usual helmet laws, then this could be one of the most successful two-wheeled vehicles ever. However, that sort of political decision, which needs to be applied by each

individual country, could take many years. The C1 is also incredibly heavy, at around 400lbs dry, which will not only restrict the speed, and particularly the acceleration of an electric variant, but put many people unused to motorcycles off the entire experience. Put simply, the C1 will still fall over on its side and some people will be afraid of having a 400lb weight landing on their leg.

Future Breeze

THE SPICESONIC SPEEDO

ABOVE: THE TRUTH IS OUT THERE: APRILIA'S AREA 51 IS PROOF

RIGHT: COMING AROUND AGAIN: A RETRO ADVERT FROM 1999

Other manufacturers are tweaking, improving and just plain re-inventing the existing scooter concept as we approach the new millennium. Honda have a new, 125cc, feet-forward-style scooter called the Pantheon, which features a clever, clean-running, two-stroke engine. The engine uses variable ignition timing so that as much of the fuel/air mixture inside the engine is burnt as possible. Most two-strokes waste fuel, throwing unburnt vapour out of their exhausts, but the Pantheon is the first of a new generation and may yet give the two-stroke engine a future.

Aprilia released their stark, futuristic-looking scooter the Area 51 in 1998. It was named after the legendary UFO research facility in the USA and certainly looked the part. Hub-centre front steering, liquid crystal instrument panel, a forward-mounted fuel cell built into the bodywork and a touch of Dan Dare space scooter in the styling department all give the Area 51 a bizarre image. But, like LCD watches in the 1980s, this styling could all be a short-lived fashion fad.

Another bizarre creation from Honda, the 1996 Joker 90 (also called the Shadow) probably shows how a fusion of retro styling and simple technology will keep the scooter in production for at least another 50 years. With its swoopy, Arlen Ness-inspired coachwork, low-slung and wide-set legshields, all topped off with pseudo-Harley-Davidson handle-bars, the Joker is a typical Japanese oddball. Yet it is still a simple runabout at heart, a fun way to shop, ride to work, or simply pose on about town like a latter-day Mod — just as with the first Vespa.

PICTURE CREDITS

The publishers would like to thank the following sources for their kind permission
to reproduce the pictures in this book:

THE ADVERTISING ARCHIVES 9TR, 15BC, 18, 19TC, 35, 42, **ALL ACTION**/JACK LUDLAM 80BR, **APRILIA MOTO (U.K.) LTD** 5TL, BR, 7, 77BL, 87, 94C, **BENELLI MOTOR** COURTESY OF MOTO CINELLI 76BC, **BMW (GB) LTD** 92, 93, **CAPITAL PICTURES**/ZED 80TL, **CORBIS**/BETTMANN 5BL, 49/UPI 26, **NIGEL COX, WESTON SCOOTER PARTS** 8TL, 25, **PATRICK COX**/ARENA MAGAZINE 78, **CREATION RECORDS** 38, **JUSTIN DOWNING** 50, **MARY EVANS PICTURE LIBRARY** 30, 32/ROGER MAYNE 52T, 52BR, **HULTON GETTY** 5TR, 10, 13BC, 16CR, 20CL, 27, 28, 29CL, 41BC, 43, 44, 45TL, 45TR, 52BL/T DISNEY 53TC, 58C, **RONALD GRANT ARCHIVE** 9TL, 20CR, 57/TCF/STANLEY DONEN 23BL, MGM 8TR, 23BR/UNIVERSAL/7PICTURES CORPORATION/RAOUL WALSH ENTERPRISES 23CB/WARNER 5TC, 11, **HARGLO-MALAGUTI** 77BR, 83T, **HONDA U.K.** 69TC, 71BC, 77T, **ITALJET U.K.** 9TC, 68, 69B, 79, 82, 84, 85, **REBECCA LEWIS** 81R, **CLIVE MILLS** 24, 33, 36, 41C, 54, **ANDREW MORLAND** 47, **DON MORLEY INTERNATIONAL SPORTS PHOTO AGENCY** 69C, ADVERTISING CREATED BY **OGILVY AND MATHER**, ON BEHALF OF IBM 95, **PA NEWS** 5BC, 19TL, 62TL, 63BL, 67/LOUISA BULLER 64BC/DAVID JONES 90/OLIVER MULTHAUP 83BC/MUFTY MUNIR 63T/REUTER PHOTOS 6, **PICTORIAL PRESS LTD**/POLYGRAM 55T, PHOTOGRAPHS COURTESY OF **PIAGGIO LIMITED** 1, 2, 3, 13TC, 14C, 15T, 19C, 19BR, 21, 22, 23TR, 23TL, 62C, 64TC, 71C, 73, 72BL, 74T, 75, 88, 89, **RETNA PICTURES** JILL FURMANOVSKY 66/CHERYL HULBERT 65/RORY MOLES 55BC, 55BL, **REX FEATURES LTD.**/STEVE FENTON 81L/PHILIP IDE 17, **SCOOTERING MAGAZINE** 12, 16CL, 31, 37, 39, 46, 51, 58BC, 60, 61, 63BR, 70, 73BL, **SUZUKI (GB) LTD** 74BR, **THREE CROSS MOTORCYCLES**, IMPORTERS OF PEUGEOT 76T, 91, **TOPHAM PICTUREPOINT** 48, 53BC, **VICTORY MOTORCYCLES**/ROGER TAYLOR-WHITE 8TC, **THE VINTAGE MAGAZINE ARCHIVE LTD.** 4, 14BC, 29CR, 34, 56, 59/POLYGRAM 55BR, **ALASTAIR WALKER** 86, **YAMAHA MOTOR U.K. LTD** 74BL

Special thanks are due to Clive Mills and Graham Perdeaux at Victory Motorcycles, London;
Richard Forde at ScooterZone Ltd, London; Bob Brennan and Mark Garner at Platinum
Motorcycles, London; Nigel Cox at Weston Scooter Parts, Weston-super-Mare; and Vanessa
Cotton at Creation Records.

AUTHOR'S ACKNOWLEDGEMENTS

Thanks to the following people for their advice, specialized knowledge and support
in making this book possible:
**Stuart Lanning and *Scootering* magazine, Gary Inman, Phil Terry,
John Bolt, Julie Walker, Robert Kerr and Corinne Ellis.**